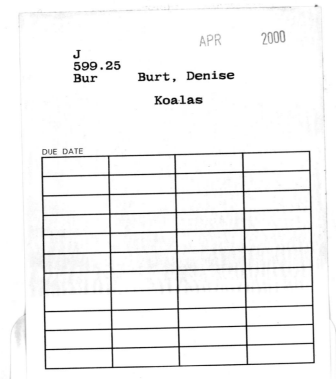

Koalas

Koalas

by Denise Burt

photographs by Neil McLeod

edited by Sylvia A. Johnson

A Carolrhoda Nature Watch Book

Carolrhoda Books, Inc. / Minneapolis

Additional photograph courtesy of: © Gary Mezaros/Visuals Unlimited, p. 9 (left).

Maps on pp. 11–12, 15 by Lejla Fazlic Omerovic, copyright © 1999 Carolrhoda Books, Inc.

This edition first published 1999 by Carolrhoda Books, Inc. Copyright © 1986 by Denise Burt. Original edition published in 1986 in Australia by Buttercup Books under the title of BIRTH OF A KOALA. Adapted for Carolrhoda Books, Inc., by Sylvia A. Johnson. Additional text for this edition © 1999 by Carolrhoda Books, Inc.

Carolrhoda Books, Inc.
A Division of the Lerner Publishing Group
241 First Avenue North, Minneapolis, MN 55401 U.S.A.

Website address: www.lernerbooks.com

LIBRARY OF CONGRESS CATALOGING-IN-PUBLICATION DATA

Burt, Denise.
    Koalas / by Denise Burt : photographs by Neil McLeod; edited by Sylvia A. Johnson.
        p.   cm.
    "A Carolrhoda nature watch book."
    Includes index.
    Summary: Describes the physical characteristics, life cycle, behavior, and conservation of koalas.
    ISBN 1-57505-380-2 (alk. paper)
    1. Koala—Juvenile literature. [1. Koala.] I. McLeod, Neil, ill. II. Johnson, Sylvia A. III. Title.
QL737.M384B875   1999
599.2'5—dc21   99-46097

Manufactured in the United States of America
1 2 3 4 5 6 – JR – 04 03 02 01 00 99

CONTENTS

A POPULAR ANIMAL

If you could ask people around the world to choose their favorite wild animals, which ones would they pick? The lion, with its powerful body and golden mane? The long-legged giraffe or the graceful antelope?

Near the top of any list of favorites, you would probably find an animal not known for its power or grace. This animal is popular for very different reasons.

It has a round body covered with soft, thick fur. Its ears are large and fluffy, and its nose is big and black. Maybe the best word to describe it is "cute." In fact, it looks a lot like a cuddly toy teddy bear.

This popular animal is, of course, the koala. A native of Australia, it is loved by people all over the world. But how much do we really know about this appealing animal?

WHAT IS A KOALA?

The first and most important thing to know about koalas is that even though they may look like teddy bears, they are not bears. They are not even related to wild bears such as the grizzly or the black bear. Instead, the koala's closest relatives are wombats and possums, small animals that live in Australia. Koalas are also related to the opossums of North and South America. On a more distant branch of the koala family tree is the kangaroo.

What all these animals have in common is a special method of producing their young. They are **marsupials** (mar-SOUP-ee-uhls), animals whose babies are born at a very early stage of development. A young koala, like most marsupial babies, finishes its development in a pouch on the outside of its mother's body. Because marsupials, like humans, are **mammals,** the growing baby koala is nourished by its mother's milk.

Most marsupials live in one part of the world—Australia and the islands surrounding it. Opossums and their relatives live thousands of miles away in North and South America. Why are these unusual animals found only in these places? The answer to this question is part of the fascinating story of Earth's history.

Left: *The Virginia opossum is a marsupial from North America.*
Right: *The wombat, a close relative of the koala, lives in Australia.*

9

A LAND OF MARSUPIALS

Modern Australia is separated from the other continents of the world, but in the distant past, this was not true. Millions of years ago, all the world's land areas were joined in one supercontinent that scientists call Pangaea. Then powerful geological forces caused this landmass to begin breaking apart. The gradual movement of enormous plates in the earth's crust started the process known as **continental drift,** which is still shaping the earth.

The first marsupials probably developed in the part of Pangaea that would eventually become North America. From there, they made their way to the future South America and then to Antarctica and Australia. Marsupials died out in North America some time after the breakup of Pangaea, about 200 million years ago. But in South America, Antarctica, and Australia—at this time part of another giant continent called Gondwana—marsupials survived.

Around 100 million years ago, South America separated from Gondwana and began moving toward its present location. Still joined, Australia and Antarctica moved gradually in the opposite direction, carrying with them marsupials as well as other early animals.

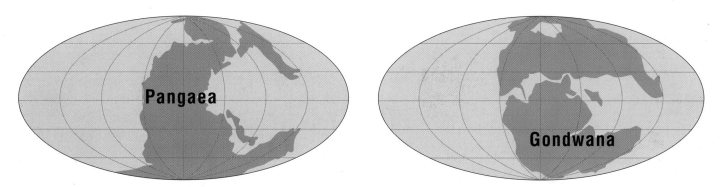

About 250 million years ago, when marsupials first appeared, all the earth's land areas were joined in one giant continent called Pangaea (left). About 200 million years ago, marsupials lived in Gondwana, a large landmass that would become the modern continents of South America, Africa, Antarctica, and Australia (right).

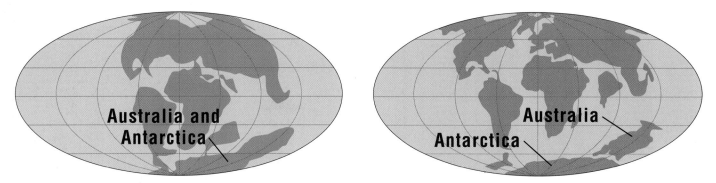

About 100 million years ago, Australia and Antarctica were joined together (left). When the two continents separated about 45 million years ago (right), Antarctica's marsupials died out, but koalas and other Australian marsupials survived.

The two landmasses separated about 45 million years ago, and Antarctica drifted closer to the cold South Pole. Its marsupials died out, but in warmer Australia, they thrived.

The marsupials in South America were not so successful. When South America rejoined North America around 3 million years ago, many different **species,** or kinds, of animals moved south. Most South American marsupials could not compete with these new species, and they became extinct, or died out forever. Only the opossums and their relatives survived. Eventually a few opossums made the return trip to North America.

(Two species of opossums are still found in the United States and Canada.)

In Australia, which was separated from the rest of the world, marsupials had little competition from other kinds of animals. Many new species evolved, or slowly developed, and soon marsupials occupied all the different kinds of environments available for animal life.

About 120 species of marsupials live in modern Australia. They range from kangaroos that stand almost 7 feet (2 m) tall to tiny marsupial moles and mice. The furry, big-eared koala is one of the best known of the Australian marsupials.

The red kangaroo (above) is a large Australian marsupial, measuring almost 7 feet (2 m) in height. The pademelon (right) is a much smaller member of the kangaroo family.

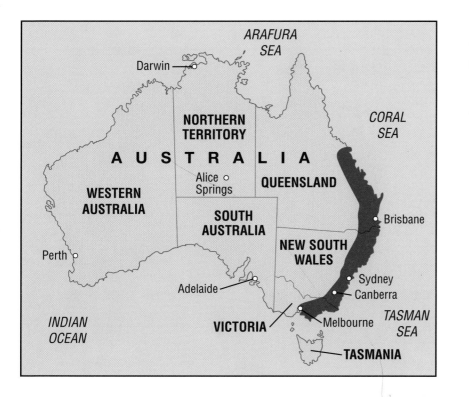

A LIFE IN THE TREES

Koalas live in a long, narrow strip of eastern Australia, near the coast of the Pacific Ocean. This area includes several different climates, and there are some differences among the koalas that make their homes there. For example, in the cool southern state of Victoria, koalas are larger and have darker, thicker fur than their relatives in the warmer north. (Because Australia is located in the Southern Hemisphere, temperatures are colder in the south than in the north.)

An average adult male koala in Victoria measures about 2½ feet (76 cm) in length and weighs as much as 30 pounds (about 14 kg). In the north, a Queensland male koala may be only 2 feet tall (about 61 cm) and weigh around 15 pounds (about 7 kg). In all areas, females are smaller than males.

Koalas make their homes in the forests of eucalyptus (you-kah-LIP-tuhs), or eucalypt, trees that grow in eastern Australia. They spend almost their entire lives high up among the branches of the trees. The eucalyptus provides food, shelter, and almost everything else the marsupials need to survive.

Koalas are well suited to their lives in the trees. They have long, powerful legs and paws with very sharp, strong claws.

A koala's claws are ideal for holding on to tree trunks and branches. The paws also have other features useful for climbing.

16

The five toes on the front paws are separated into two sections, one made up of two toes and the other of three. A koala can use these two sets of toes to hold and grip, similar to the way a person holds things with the thumb and fingers.

Front paw

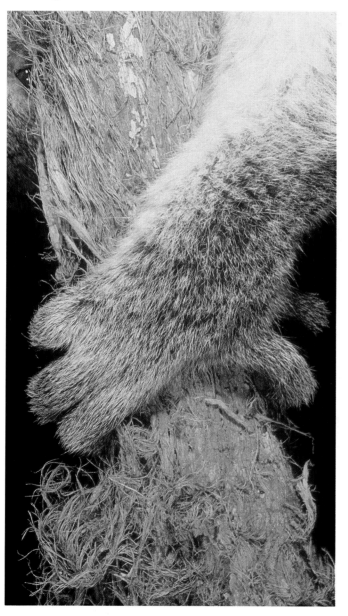

Back paw

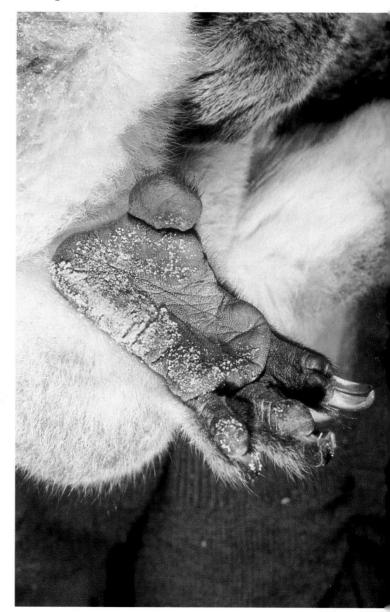

Above: *A koala grooms its fur with the joined toes on its back foot.*
Opposite: *This koala lives in a cool part of Australia and has thicker fur than its relatives in warmer areas.*

The toes on a koala's back paws are also unusual. There is a round "big toe" without a claw and three other toes, two of which are joined along most of their length. These joined toes are used in grooming. A koala combs them through its thick fur to keep it clean and fluffy.

Even with large babies on their backs, these female koalas have no trouble climbing in the trees.

Because koalas are **arboreal** (ar-BOR-ee-uhl), or tree-dwelling, animals, they spend very little time on the ground. They move around by leaping from branch to branch or from tree to tree. To reach a distant tree, they climb down from their perch rear end first, clinging to the trunk with their sharp claws.

A koala on the ground walks on all four legs, swaying awkwardly from side to side. If necessary, the marsupial can run, bringing its hind legs forward in a kind of gallop. When it reaches its new destination, a koala grabs on to the tree trunk with its powerful claws. Moving first its front legs and then its hind legs, it scoots up the trunk to the safety of the treetops.

Opposite: *Koalas walk on all four feet. They are less graceful on the ground than when swinging through the trees.*
Right: *Wedged between two tree branches, a female koala and her baby get ready for a nap.*

What do koalas do while they are perched high in the branches of a eucalyptus tree? Most of the time, they sleep. The average koala spends about 18 hours of each day sleeping or resting. And since koalas are **nocturnal** (nock-TURN-uhl) animals, active mainly at night, most of this dozing takes place during the daylight hours.

Koalas don't make nests or platforms for sleeping. They usually wedge themselves between forks in tree branches or between a branch and the tree trunk. The thick layers of fur and fat on their rear ends make good pads for sitting on hard wood.

In cool or windy weather, koalas sleep huddled up. When the weather is hot, a koala often stretches out on a branch with its stomach exposed. Because the fur on its stomach is a lighter color than the fur on the rest of its body, it reflects heat. In rainy weather, a koala's thick fur sheds water and keeps the marsupial dry.

When koalas are not sleeping, they are usually eating or looking for food. They do not have to look far, since their diet is made up almost entirely of eucalyptus leaves. If absolutely necessary, koalas will eat the leaves of other trees, but their first choice is always eucalyptus.

About 600 different kinds of eucalyptus trees grow in the eastern part of Australia. Their leaves are thick, oily, and full of plant fiber. They are also low in nutrition and contain poisons that make most animals sick. But koalas are able to survive on this unusual diet.

Koalas are very picky when it comes to selecting their leafy food. They normally eat the leaves of only about 50 to 60 kinds of eucalyptus trees. They choose their meals carefully, sniffing the leaves and looking for those that are young and tender. Their strong front teeth nip the leaves from the branches, and the back teeth grind them into a green pulp.

A koala's digestive system is well suited to this leafy diet. It has a special chamber called the **caecum** (SEE-kum), in which leaves go through extra processing to extract all the nutrients they contain.

Adult koalas usually eat about 2 pounds (a little less than 1 kg) of eucalyptus leaves each day. But the low food value of their diet does not provide them with a lot of energy. This is one of the reasons koalas move slowly and spend much of their time sleeping.

Koalas get most of the moisture they need from dew on the eucalyptus leaves and from the leaves themselves. They very seldom take a drink of water. According to one theory, koalas got their name because of this characteristic. The name *koala* may come from a word that means "drinks no water" in a language spoken by the Aborigines (a-bor-IJ-in-ees), the native people of Australia.

Koalas get most of the moisture they need from eucalyptus leaves.

LIVING ALONE

Koalas are not very social animals. They do not live together in groups or families. A young koala stays with its mother for about a year and then goes off on its own. But even while living alone in the eucalyptus forest, koalas have ways of keeping in touch.

Scientists who study koalas have found that each adult in a particular region has a **home range.** This special area contains enough eucalyptus trees to supply the koala with food and shelter. The animal usually stays in its home range for most of its life, moving from tree to tree in search of fresh leaves.

A koala marks the trees around the boundary of its home range to let other koalas know where this special place is. It scratches the tree trunks with its sharp claws. A male koala has another way of marking trees on the borders of his territory. He rubs them with a smelly liquid produced by a **scent gland** in the middle of his chest. Female koalas do not have scent glands.

A young koala (top) *with its mother. It will soon leave to begin life on its own.*

Usually one male will have a larger home range than neighboring koalas. He is the **dominant** male in the area, and the borders of his home range often overlap the home ranges of several females. When the mating season arrives, he will probably mate with these nearby females.

Left: *An adult male koala.*
Opposite: *You can see this female koala's pouch between her hind legs. Unlike the pouches of many other marsupials, a koala's pouch opens from the rear.*

MATING AND HAVING YOUNG

Female koalas are ready to mate and have young when they are about two years old. Males are also able to reproduce at this age. Because they have to be large and strong enough to compete with other male koalas, however, they usually don't mate until they are four or five.

The koala mating season is September through March, which are the spring and summer months in Australia. During this period, the bellowing of male koalas can be heard all through the night in the eucalyptus forest. People say that this loud noise sounds something like a pig snorting or a motorcycle engine starting.

A male koala bellows to let females know where he is and to tell rival males to stay away. If bellowing doesn't work, male koalas will sometimes fight over mates.

Once a male and female find each other, they mate high up in the treetops. Then the male koala leaves to look for other partners, while the female gets ready to have her young.

A female koala usually has only one baby at a time. The young koala grows inside its mother's body for only 35 days. At birth, it is still in a very early stage of development. It is not much bigger than a bean and weighs much less than 1 ounce (about half a gram).

The baby koala has no hair and cannot see or hear. Its back legs are just starting to take shape, but its front legs are well developed and already have strong claws. The baby uses those strong legs and claws to get to its mother's pouch.

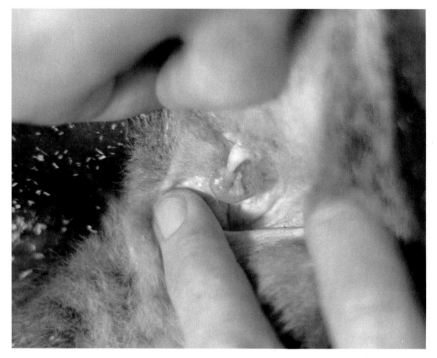

A baby koala at one day old (above) *and at ten days old* (below)

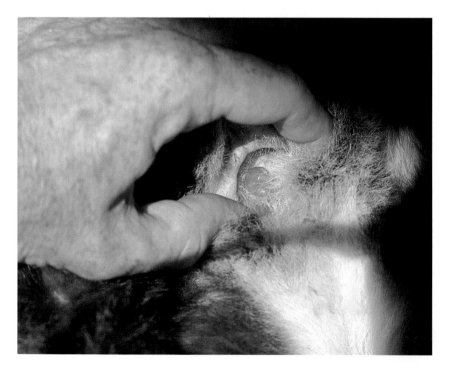

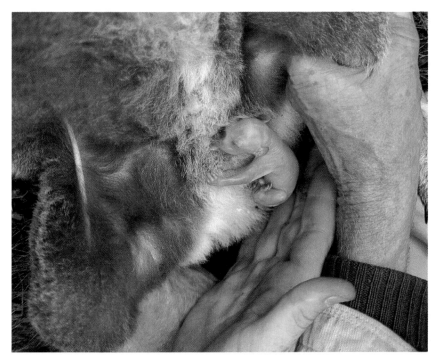

At two months (above), *a young koala is blind and furless. By four months* (below), *its eyes have still not opened, but its back legs have developed.*

After emerging from the birth canal, the blind little creature clings to the fur on its mother's stomach. Guided by its sense of smell, it pulls itself along until it reaches the safety of the pouch. The mother koala does not help her youngster during this journey, which takes about five minutes. If the baby falls off, it will have no chance of surviving.

Once inside the pouch, a baby koala finds one of its mother's two **teats,** or nipples, and begins to drink milk. It will spend the next four months of its life holding onto the teat and nursing, while its development continues.

A YOUNG KOALA GROWS

At five months, a baby koala's eyes are open, and it has a coat of fur.

With a constant supply of nourishing milk, the baby koala grows rapidly. Its back legs develop, and its fur starts to appear. When it is about five months old, its eyes open, and it sometimes peeks out of the pouch opening.

Around this time, the young koala starts feeding on a special food supplied by its mother. In addition to milk, the baby eats something called **pap**. This soft material, made up of partly digested leaves, comes out of the mother's **anus** (AY-nuhs), the opening at the lower end of the digestive tract.

Leaning out of the pouch, the baby koala feeds on this nourishing food, which contains tiny organisms from the mother's digestive system. These organisms play an important role in the digestion of eucalyptus leaves. When the baby eats pap, it takes these useful organisms into its own body. It will feed on this special food for several weeks, growing bigger and stronger every day.

When a young koala is about six months old, its fur is fully developed, and its first teeth start to appear. It is finally ready to spend some time outside its mother's pouch. It clings to the fur on the mother's stomach, hanging on with its strong claws. But the baby returns to the pouch often to drink milk and to sleep.

At about seven months, the young koala has almost become too big to fit into the pouch. At this stage, it rides around on its mother's back, going wherever she goes.

When it is around six months old, a young koala comes out of its mother's pouch for the first time.

*A koala mother
with twins*

The koala mother in this picture has two young ones on her back. It is very unusual for a female koala to have twins. Although the pouch has two teats, there is not enough room inside it for two growing babies. If twins are born, one of them usually does not survive.

This mother koala lives in a wildlife reserve, where she had help raising her young. A wildlife officer fed and cared for one of the babies, and both survived. Soon they will be ready to find food for themselves.

A young koala learns to eat eucalyptus leaves by following its mother's example.

As a mother koala feeds among the branches of the trees, the youngster riding on her back also nibbles on eucalyptus leaves. Gradually it learns how to find leaves by smell and how to select the tastiest ones.

When a young koala grows up, it usually eats the same kind of eucalyptus leaves that its mother ate. The early lessons in finding food last a lifetime.

At about nine months, a young koala begins to leave its mother for short periods of time. It stays near her in the trees but climbs around by itself, looking for food. The young koala may come back from time to time for a drink of milk. When it is about one year old, however, it has to start living on its own. Its mother has another young one developing in her pouch, and she has no time for last year's baby.

Opposite: *Even after a young koala is full grown, it will sometimes try to climb onto its mother's back.*
Above: *These young koalas are ready to begin lives of their own.*

After a young koala leaves its mother, it often stays in her home range for another year. Then it is time to go. If the young one is a female, she usually tries to establish a home range near that of her mother. Young males wander around for several years before looking for a place to settle down and call their own.

In the past, young koalas could find many areas of eucalyptus forest in which to live. In modern Australia, however, living space is becoming scarce, and koalas face an uncertain future.

THE FUTURE FOR KOALAS

Koalas have lived in Australia for thousands of years. In the past, Aborigines hunted the marsupials for their fur and meat. Koalas also played an important role in the stories and legends that Aborigines told about the natural world. Like the bison in North America, the koala was both a source of food and an animal respected for its supernatural power.

When Europeans came to Australia in the late 1700s, they were amazed by the continent's unusual animal life. Early settlers thought that the koala was a peculiar kind of monkey or sloth, but they were very impressed by its thick fur. By the late 1800s, a thriving trade in koala fur had grown up in Australia. Millions of koalas were trapped or poisoned, and their skins were shipped to Great Britain and the United States.

Largely because of the fur trade, koalas disappeared in some parts of Australia. People began to protest the loss of this unique animal, and gradually hunting koalas for their fur was made illegal. The last "open season" took place in 1927, when nearly 600,000 koalas were killed.

After the fur trade was ended, the koala population in many areas began to grow. But soon koalas faced another threat. Like so many animals around the world, they were gradually losing their living space to humans.

As the Australian population grew in the mid-1900s, eucalyptus forests were cut down to make way for farms and towns. The loss of forests has continued as the eastern part of Australia becomes more and more developed.

Even in areas where eucalyptus forests survive, koalas can't live in complete safety. Often the forests are near human settlements, with their houses and highways. When the marsupials try to walk across roads, which are often built right through their home ranges, they are hit by cars. The animals are also attacked and killed by pet dogs.

Even backyard swimming pools can be a threat. Koalas can swim, but if a koala falls into a pool, it is often unable to climb out and eventually drowns.

Despite these threats, most scientists do not think that koalas are in danger of extinction at this time. In fact, no one really knows exactly how many koalas are left in Australia. Because the animals spend most of their time in the treetops, it is difficult for scientists to see and count them.

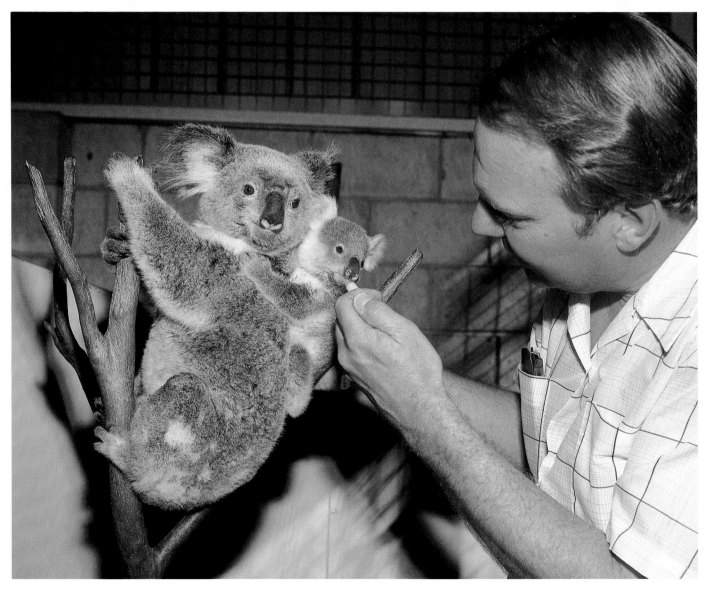

Some koalas are protected in wildlife reserves. This baby koala is being fed by a veterinarian.

While they are not in immediate danger, koalas face some very serious problems. Australians are deeply concerned about the lovable marsupial, which has become a symbol of their country. They have built hospitals where injured koalas can receive care. They have formed organizations dedicated to the protection of koalas and of the eucalyptus forests. In some parts of Australia, governments have established parks and refuges where koalas can live undisturbed by people.

But what about the future? Eucalyptus forests are still being cut down. If their natural homes are destroyed, koalas may be able to survive only in refuges and wildlife parks.

People in Australia and all over the world don't want to see this happen. They hope that koalas will continue living in freedom and safety among the eucalyptus trees.

GLOSSARY

anus: the opening at the lower end of the digestive tract through which wastes are eliminated. Female koalas also excrete a special food for their young through this opening.

arboreal: living in the trees

caecum: a section of a koala's digestive system in which leaves are broken down to extract all the nutrients they contain

continental drift: the gradual change in the position of continents caused by movement of enormous plates in the earth's crust. Continental drift is part of the scientific theory of plate tectonics (tek-TON-iks).

dominant: taking first place in a group of animals. A dominant male koala usually has a larger home range than other koalas in the area and mates with more females than the other males.

home range: a specific area in which a koala lives and finds food. Koalas mark the boundaries of their home ranges to let other koalas know where these special areas are.

mammals: animals that feed their young with milk produced by mammary glands. Koalas, kangaroos, and opossums are marsupial mammals; humans belong to a different group known as placental (plah-SENT-uhl) mammals.

marsupials: animals whose young are born in a very early stage of development. A marsupial baby finishes its growth in a pouch on the outside of its mother's body.

nocturnal: active mainly at night

pap: partly digested leaves excreted by mother koalas to feed their young. Pap contains organisms from the mother's body that young koalas need to digest leaves.

scent gland: a structure on the chest of a male koala that produces a smelly liquid used to mark territory

species: a group of animals or plants with many characteristics in common

teats: the nipples from which a young mammal sucks milk

INDEX

ABOUT THE AUTHOR

Denise Burt is an author and publisher, with a very strong interest in the flora and fauna of her Australian homeland. She has had numerous children's books published, as well as educational material for classroom use. She lives with her husband in suburban Melbourne but plans eventually to live in the country.

ABOUT THE PHOTOGRAPHER

Neil McLeod is a man of many interests. He is a nature photographer, painter, publisher, naturalist, and adventurer. He travels a lot in outback Australia, living and working with Aborigines to observe their customs and to add to his already extensive knowledge. He has published over thirty books about Australia and its native animals.